A fashionable HISTORY *of* MAKE-UP & BODY DECORATION

A FASHIONABLE HISTORY OF MAKE-UP &
BODY DECORATION
was produced by

David West ☆ᴀ̊ᴋ **Children's Books**
7 Princeton Court
55 Felsham Road
London SW15 1AZ

Author: Helen Reynolds
Editor: Jackie Gaff
Picture Research: Carlotta Cooper
Designer: Julie Joubinaux

First published in Great Britain in 2003 by
Heinemann Library, Halley Court, Jordan Hill,
Oxford OX2 8EJ, a division of
Harcourt Education Ltd.

OXFORD MELBOURNE AUCKLAND
JOHANNESBURG BLANTYRE GABORONE
IBADAN PORTSMOUTH (NH) USA CHICAGO

Copyright © 2003 David West Children's Books

07 06 05 04 03
10 9 8 7 6 5 4 3 2 1

ISBN 0 431 18330 9 (HB)
ISBN 0 431 18338 4 (PB)

British Library Cataloguing in Publication Data

Reynolds, Helen
A fashionable history of make up and body
decoration
1. Cosmetics - History - Juvenile literature
2. Body marking - History - Juvenile literature
3. Fashion - History - Juvenile literature
I. Title II. Make up and body decoration
391.6'3'09

Printed and bound in China

PHOTO CREDITS :
Abbreviations: t-top, m-middle, b-bottom, r-right,
l-left, c-centre.

Front cover m & 10l, tl & 12bl, r & 18l and
pages 5tr, 6br, 10br, 11tr, 12tl & r, 16tr, 17tl &
tr, 20-21, 23l, 24tl, 25r & 26bl – Mary Evans
Picture Library.
Pages 3, 4br, 5br, 6-7t, 16bl, 19bl, 24tr & b, 25tl –
Dover Books. 4tr, 6tl & bl, 9tr, 22br, 26r, 28bl, 29r
& b – The Culture Archive. 5l, 7 all, 8ml, 9bl &
br, 11tl & br, 13tl & br, 14l & tr, 15tl & br, 17bl,
18tr, 19tr & br, 20tr, 21 & br, 22bl, 23br, 25bl,
27tr & br, 28-29 – Rex Features Ltd. 8tl – The
Kobal Collection/BFI/United Artists. 14-15 – The
Kobal Collection/ICON/Ladd Co./Paramount. 8bl –
Hulton Archive. 11b – Corbis Images. 13tr, 27l –
Digital Stock. 20tl – ISG113867 A Young Lady of
Fashion (oil on panel) by Paolo Uccello (1397-
1475), Isabella Stewart Gardner Museum, Boston,
Massachusetts, USA/Bridgeman Art Library. 22tr –
(LDBDA s236 – Elephant ivory dentures featuring
human, or 'Waterloo' teeth, and human teeth
strung together for sale, 1815-20) & m (LDBDA
s301 – "A French dentist shewing a specimen of his
artificial teeth and false palates", 1785, Thomas
Rowlandson caricaturing Nicholas Dubois de
Chémant) – British Dental Association Museum
Collection.

Every effort has been made to contact copyright
holders of any material reproduced in this book.
Any omissions will be rectified in subsequent
printings if notice is given to the publishers.

*An explanation of difficult words can be
found in the glossary on page 31.*

A *fashionable* HISTORY of MAKE-UP & BODY DECORATION

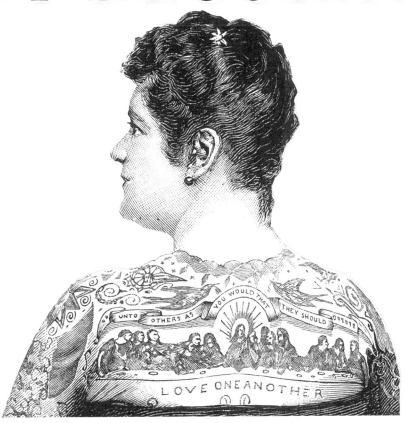

UNTO OTHERS AS YOU WOULD THAT THEY SHOULD

LOVE ONEANOTHER

Heinemann
LIBRARY

Contents

*A*NCIENT ADORNMENT

Women and men were beautifying themselves with make-up back in ancient Egyptian times.

*M*AKING A LASTING IMPRESSION

Although the tattooist's art is at least 5,000 years old, its revived popularity in the West dates from the 1760s. Illustrated men and women with the kind of all-over tattoo shown below were popular exhibits at fairgrounds and circuses in the early 19th century.

From eye-paint to illustrated skin

A STROLL DOWN A BUSY STREET *in any of the world's major cities will today reveal countless variations in face and body decoration. Most people now take experimenting with their appearance for granted. The presence or absence of make-up is widely accepted, as are tattoos and body piercing. Body decoration is not a modern phenomenon, however, and it has meant different things in different cultures throughout history. Among other things, make-up has been employed as a badge of social status and to proclaim membership of a group. Above all, though, it has been used to enhance beauty, with every era setting its own standard of fashionable perfection.*

MAKE-UP FOR THE MASSES

In the 1920s, mass production made cosmetics more widely available.

CUTTING A FINE FIGURE

Fashions in facial hair have fluctuated over the years. In the early 1900s, the stylish Edwardian swell sported a big, bushy moustache.

HOME-COOKED BEAUTY AIDS

Caring for the skin has always been as important as covering it up with make-up. Recipes that use kitchen-cupboard ingredients to whip up face packs and skin ointments have been around since ancient times.

The eyes have it

EYE-PAINTS DATE BACK TO ANTIQUITY *and originally may have been used as a form of magical eye protection. By ancient Egyptian times, however, vanity had taken over and eye-paints were used by both men and women as beauty aids.*

Mice in the make-up box

Ideas about eye beauty changed over the centuries, with some bizarre practices coming and going. In the 18th century, for instance, fashionable women shaved off their eyebrows and applied artificial ones made from mouseskin!

EGYPTIAN BEAUTY SECRETS

Egyptian eye-paints were made from minerals ground into powder. Eyes were either outlined in kohl made from black galena (a lead ore) or with green malachite (a copper ore).

ELIZABETHAN EYESORE

Queen Elizabeth 1 (1533–1603) used drops of the poisonous deadly nightshade plant (below) to make her pupils larger and her eyes appear more brilliant. Fashionable women continued this practice for centuries afterwards.

NEW TAKE ON AN OLD LOOK

This American magazine feature illustrated the 1960s fashion for Egyptian-style eye make-up in heavy kohl pencil.

Victorian values give way to flapper freedoms

By the 19th century, the obvious use of make-up was frowned upon and it was only worn by the kind of women considered disreputable, such as actresses and prostitutes. The early 20th century saw huge changes in women's lives, however, and an accompanying shake-up in acceptable behaviour.

The short hair and cloche hats of the 1920s flapper girl drew attention to the face. Eyes were highlighted with an eyebrow pencil and coloured eyeshadow, as well as lashings of dark mascara.

In the following decades the emphasis was more on the lips, but as skirts shrank in the 1960s, eyes became big again – literally. Mini-skirted chicks accentuated their eyes with opalescent eye shadow, false eyelashes and thick, black eyeliner.

CLOSE EYE CONTACT

Coloured and patterned contact lenses (above) were a late 20th-century introduction – another way of emphasizing the eyes.

MODEL MAKE-UP

With her dark, heavily made-up eyes, pale lips and short, geometric haircut, the fashion model Twiggy (Leslie Hornby b.1949) was the epitome of 1960s glamour.

LUSCIOUS LASHES

Although at their most popular in the 1960s and 1970s, false eyelashes have been around since the early 1900s.

Painted Men

In the 18th century, upper-class men and women wore elaborate make-up, including lip-paints made from ground-up plaster of Paris with added colourings.

Pretty Boys

The 1980s saw a general trend towards glitz and glamour. In subcultures such as the New Romantics, men and women wore lashings of bold make-up, including dramatic lipstick.

Rebel, Rebel

Although during much of the 19th century make-up was frowned upon, from the 1890s onwards, suffragettes campaigning for votes for women sometimes adopted red lip-paint. It was a symbol of their defiance of traditional ideas about acceptable female behaviour.

Lovely lips

LIP-PAINT IS ANOTHER BEAUTY AID that dates back to ancient times. Neatly packaged lipsticks weren't available in those days, of course, and cosmetics were made by the wearer or a servant. The ancient Egyptians ground up an earth called red ochre, while the Greeks mashed up seaweed and mulberries.

Nature & artifice

Bold use of lip-paint went in and out of vogue over the years. Roman women loved bright lips, for example, while in the Middle Ages a more natural look was preferred.

In 17th- and 18th-century Europe, lip-paints were used by the nobility of both sexes, as a mark of their social rank. After the French Revolution of 1789–99, however, Europe was swept by a new passion for simplicity in clothing and general appearance.

Men stopped wearing lip-paint, and there was a sharp decline in its use by women which continued throughout much of the Victorian era.

Lip stuff

The twist-up lipstick in a metal tube was a 20th-century introduction. Before then, lip-paint mainly came in pots and was applied with the finger or a brush.

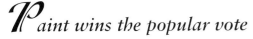

*P*aint wins the popular vote

By the early 20th century, discreet lip-paint was again being used by society ladies. Lip-crayons had been around since the 16th century, but most lip-paints came in pots, were greasy and needed a deft hand to apply them. In 1915 the first lipstick in a sliding metal tube was patented. This easy-to-apply product was an immediate success and was soon being manufactured in a range of red tints. By the 1920s the wearing of lipstick was commonplace among stylish women, and has remained so until the present day.

*R*ED FOR VICTORY

New clothes were in short supply during World War II (1939–45), so women used make-up to boost morale and add glamour to their lives.

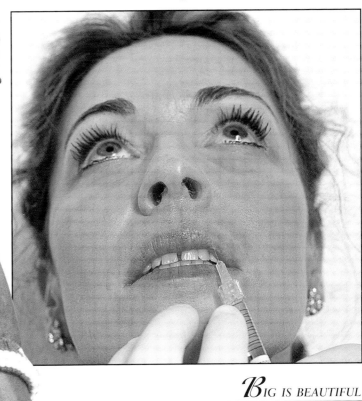

*B*IG IS BEAUTIFUL

Lip-paint isn't the only way of drawing attention to the lips. In some cultures (left), huge plugs are used to stretch them. In others (above), people have their lips injected with a substance called collagen.

The painted face

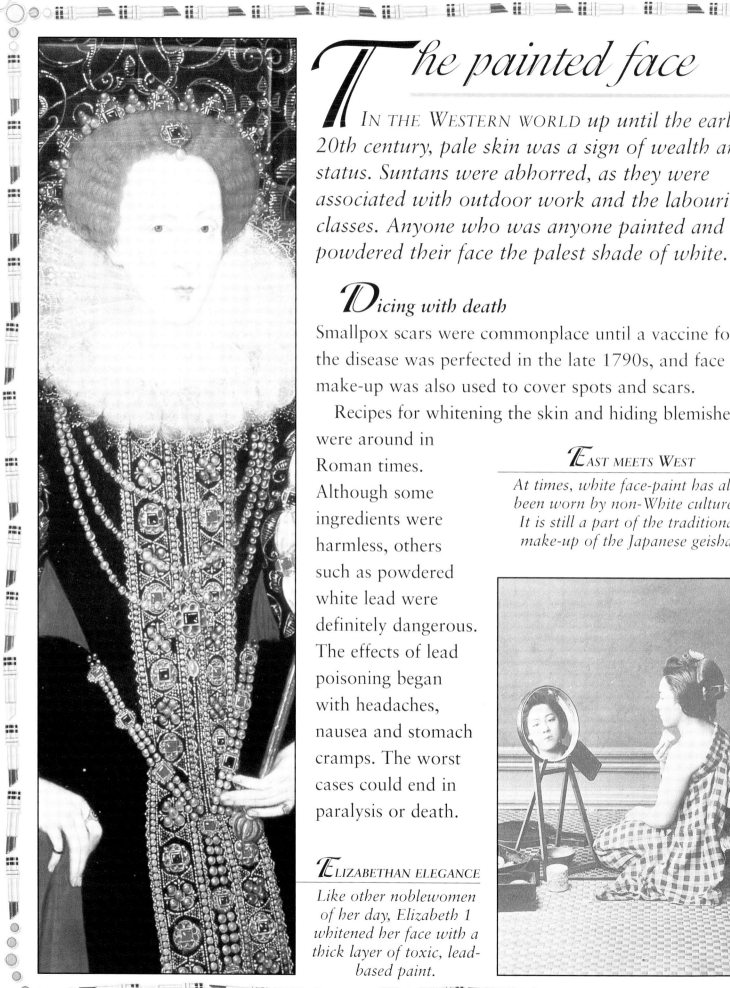

IN THE WESTERN WORLD up until the early 20th century, pale skin was a sign of wealth and status. Suntans were abhorred, as they were associated with outdoor work and the labouring classes. Anyone who was anyone painted and powdered their face the palest shade of white.

Dicing with death

Smallpox scars were commonplace until a vaccine for the disease was perfected in the late 1790s, and face make-up was also used to cover spots and scars.

Recipes for whitening the skin and hiding blemishes were around in Roman times. Although some ingredients were harmless, others such as powdered white lead were definitely dangerous. The effects of lead poisoning began with headaches, nausea and stomach cramps. The worst cases could end in paralysis or death.

ELIZABETHAN ELEGANCE

Like other noblewomen of her day, Elizabeth 1 whitened her face with a thick layer of toxic, lead-based paint.

EAST MEETS WEST

At times, white face-paint has also been worn by non-White cultures. It is still a part of the traditional make-up of the Japanese geisha.

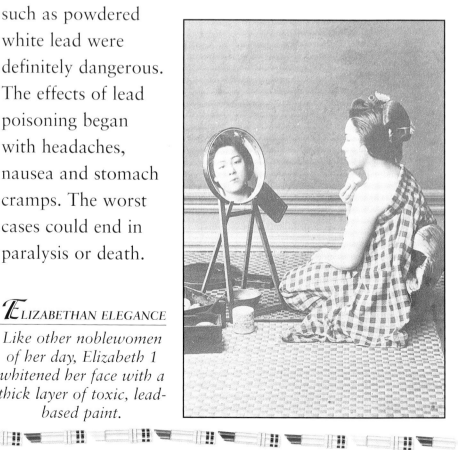

Masked beauty

Early 20th-century cosmetics such as Max Factor's Pan-Cake brand coated the skin and created a rather mask-like effect. The skin tones were naturalistic, but the look was almost as artificial as the white face-paint of earlier eras.

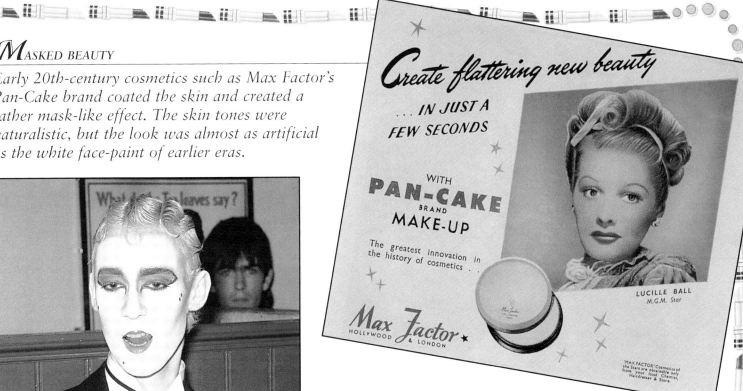

Create flattering new beauty

...IN JUST A FEW SECONDS

WITH **PAN-CAKE** BRAND **MAKE-UP**

The greatest innovation in the history of cosmetics...

LUCILLE BALL
M.G.M. Star

Max Factor★
HOLLYWOOD & LONDON

'MAX FACTOR' Cosmetics of the Stars are obtainable only from your local Chemist, Hairdresser & Store.

Ghostly white

Although flesh-coloured make-up has dominated fashion since the early 20th century, the white-faced look has sometimes resurfaced, such as in the look of the New Romantics of the 1980s.

Ending the cover-up

It wasn't until make-up fell from favour in the 19th century that the use of harmful products such as white lead declined. When make-up came back in vogue in the early 20th century, a more natural look became stylish and women began wearing flesh-coloured cosmetics. Early foundations and powders still tended to cover up the skin, creating a heavy, matt surface. It wasn't until the 1980s that sheerer, more light-reflective products became available.

Painted warriors

Face-paints have long been used in war – either as a very visible message of defiance (above) or to camouflage soldiers (left) and help them blend into the background.

Finishing touches

NOWADAYS WE USE BLUSHER to give cheeks a rosy glow. In the 17th and 18th century, noblemen and women smeared on a red paste called rouge, to create a look that to modern eyes appears more feverish than healthy.

CHEERY CHEEKS

No 18th-century lady's make-up was complete without a liberal application of rouge.

Patching over the cracks

Smallpox scars and other blemishes were hidden beneath black patches designed to look like natural beauty spots. In 18th-century Britain, patches were also used by the nobility to indicate which political party they supported. Tories wore patches on their left cheek, while their opponents, the Whigs, wore them on the right.

A PASSION FOR PATCHES

Originally used to cover blemishes, beauty patches became more elaborate in the 18th century and were cut into stars, hearts and other shapes.

DESPERATE MEASURES

To achieve a fashionable pallor, some Victorian ladies resorted to having themselves injected with dangerous substances peddled by quack chemists.

PUNK PATTERNING

In the 1970s, punks took the art of face decoration to new extremes, using everything from paints to piercing.

In countries such as India it is traditional for Hindus to make a coloured mark on the forehead as a sign of piety. In the past, married women often wore red marks, while unmarried ones had black marks. Today, the marks often match the colour of the woman's sari.

NATURAL BEAUTY

In the 1950s, women used eyebrow pencils to copy the natural beauty spots of film stars Marilyn Monroe (1926– 62) left, and Elizabeth Taylor (b.1932).

From pallor to perfection

By the 1790s the passion for patches was fading, while only older women and actresses continued to apply rouge. For much of the 19th century it was fashionable for ladies to look 'pale and interesting', with only a slight pink tinge in the cheeks – a state that was induced by avoiding fresh air and dubious practices such as drinking vinegar.

The revived popularity of make-up in the early 20th century was accompanied by a renewed interest in rouge, which was now considerably lighter in both colour and consistency and often came in powdered form.

Painted bodies

BODY PAINTING WAS PROBABLY THE EARLIEST FORM of *human artistic expression, along with cave art. It was practised by a diverse range of cultures and on most continents, from the Americas to Australia. We cannot be certain why prehistoric people developed this art, but one reason may have been to mark momentous occasions in life.*

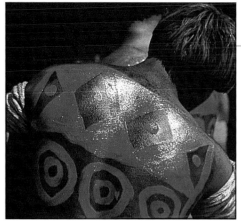

ALL DRESSED UP

In some cultures body paint is seen as a form of clothing – people would feel naked without it.

TIMELESS TRADITION

Body art has deep spiritual significance for the Aboriginal peoples of Australia, and many communities have their own unique patterns.

Rites of passage

Body art may have been used to mark a person's death and departure to the afterlife, for example, or to give symbolic protection when undertaking a difficult hunt or journey. Traditionally, the paints were made out of berries, bark, leaves and earths such as red and yellow ochre, which were ground and then mixed with vegetable oils or animal fat.

HIPPIE PROTEST

In the 1960s, some hippies adopted body paint in order to differentiate themselves from mainstream Western society.

Art & society

In some cultures, body art was seen as a way of distinguishing humans from animals. It was also used as a sign of social rank, and to separate one tribe from another.

Other cultures have practised body art for different reasons. Face-painting has long been an essential part of the circus clown's art, for instance, while performance artists have been using their own bodies as a canvas since the late 1960s. For children, having their face painted like an animal or a pirate is just part of the fun of dressing up, and face-painting stalls are now a frequent sight at fêtes and shopping centres.

BLUE FUNK

The Celtic peoples of ancient Britain made a blue body paint from the leaves of the woad plant. They used it to make themselves look even more terrifying in battle, as seen on Mel Gibson in Braveheart (1995).

BROWN STUDY

In India (right) and North Africa, the plant dye henna has been used for centuries to create highly elaborate body art for weddings and other ceremonies. Henna is now often used for temporary tattoos.

Body scarring & piercing

MORE PERMANENT THAN BODY PAINTING, scarring and piercing have also been practised for centuries. The reasons for these body arts varied between cultures, and included marking social rank or the passage into adulthood.

Making a lasting impression

Scarring techniques differed, but they often involved scratching patterns into the skin with a sharp object such as a stone or a shell. An irritant such as wood ash was then rubbed into the cuts so that raised bumps and ridges were left after the skin healed.

MARKED MAN

Although rarely done today, body scarring was traditional among Australian Aboriginals.

Taking a piercing interest

Body piercing was far more widespread than scarring, and it was carried out on virtually every part of the body. The ornaments that were inserted were made from metal, bone, shell, ivory or glass. In ancient Egypt, even cats wore earrings. Lip-plugs were worn by the Mayans of ancient Mexico and the Inuit of Alaska. Nose-rings have long been traditional in India, Pakistan and many other countries.

NOSING AROUND

Piercing the septum, or centre of the nose, was most common among warrior cultures. Nose-plugs could be as thick as 2.5 centimetres.

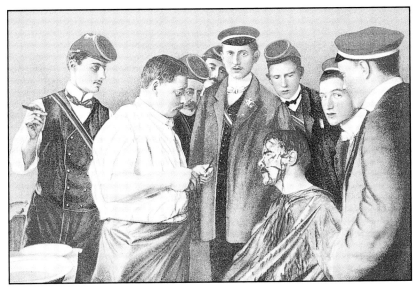

BATTLE SCARS

Until the beginning of the 20th century, German university students settled quarrels by fighting sword duels. Duelling scars were a sign of manhood and were worn with pride.

SOCIAL STIGMA

In Europe, branding scars were used to set criminals apart from the rest of society from ancient times to the early 19th century.

Ringing the changes

In mainstream fashion, over the past few hundred years, earrings were the most common reason for body piercing. It was no surprise, then, that people reacted with shocked horror in the 1970s, when punks began piercing other body parts with safety-pins. The shock didn't last long, however, and nose, eyebrow, lip, tongue and navel piercing is now widely accepted – and widely practised by young people the world over.

TAKING A TIP FROM ANCIENT HISTORY

When punks took up multiple ear-piercing, they revived a practice that archaeological evidence shows was around 4,000 years ago.

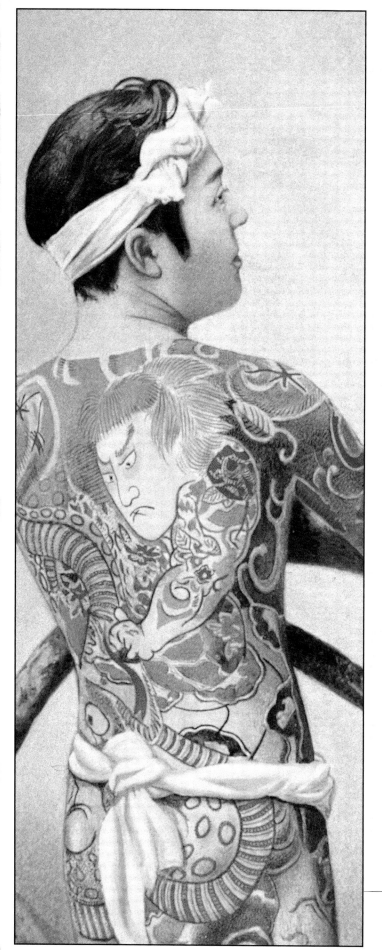

Tasty tattoos

TATTOOING IS ANOTHER PERMANENT FORM OF BODY ART, *a cross between painting and scarring. Patterns are made by pricking tiny holes, through which coloured pigments seep into the skin. In the past, tattoos were done by hand, using a sharp stick, bone or needle. In the early 1890s, the practice was revolutionized by the invention of the electric tattoo machine.*

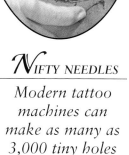

Nifty needles

Modern tattoo machines can make as many as 3,000 tiny holes per minute.

Icemen & mummies

Like other forms of body art, tattoos have meant different things to different cultures, from the purely decorative to signpointing high or low social status. One of the oldest-known examples of tattooed skin was found on the body of Utzi the Iceman, who died more than 5,200 years ago in the Alps mountains between Italy and Austria. Tattoos have also been discovered on 4,000-year-old Egyptian mummies.

The art of the Japanese tattooist

In Japan, tattooing began to flourish as an art form in the 18th century. Inspiration for the elaborate images came from woodcuts and watercolours.

Temporary tattoos

Henna is not the only form of temporary tattoo, stick-on tattoos are also available. They usually last for one to two weeks.

Sailors & pop stars

In the West, interest in tattoos was revived by the voyages of Captain James Cook (1728–79) into the Pacific during the 1760s and 1770s. Fascinated by Pacific customs, some of Cook's crew were themselves tattooed and began a trend among sailors. Tattooing is now seen as a skilled art form, particularly as practised in Japan and by the Maoris of New Zealand – and is enjoying a revival, especially among young people.

Maori messages

Called Ta Moko, the traditional Maori tattoo records a man or woman's family history as well as their tribal status.

Roll up, roll up

Although common among Western sailors by the early 19th century, tattoos were seen as highly exotic by most landlubbers. Tattooed women and men were a popular exhibit at fairgrounds and circuses, and people paid good money to gasp and stare.

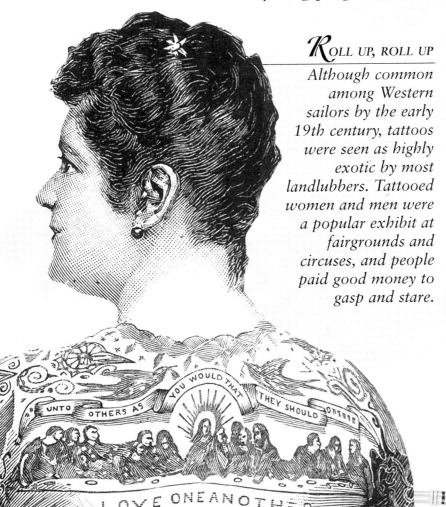

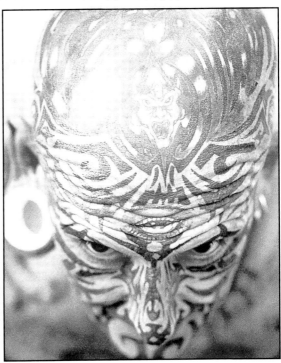

Preparation makes perfect

Modern tattooists usually work out complex designs like this on paper. A stencil is used to transfer the design and act as a guide when tattooing.

HIGH SOCIETY

During the 15th century, European noblewomen shaved their hair and sometimes their eyebrows to achieve a fashionably high forehead.

The body beautiful

IN EACH CULTURE AND ERA, people have had different ideas about beauty. In the West in the late 19th century, for instance, women used corsets and bottom-enlarging bustles to create voluptuous S-shaped curves. In the 1920s and 1960s, the stylish women's figure was boyishly flat-chested.

Bound head & foot

In some cultures, the pursuit of the perfect body shape led to more permanent changes. In China, until the custom was banned in 1911, young girls' feet were bound to restrict their growth to as little as 8 centimetres. In some African and North American communities, the practice of head-shaping dates back hundreds of years.

Head start

In the past, the Chinook people of northwestern North America practised head-shaped by strapping their childrens' heads between wooden planks.

Neck bands

Among the Padaung tribe of Burma, an elongated neck was considered beautiful for women. Gold or copper neck-rings were added over a period of time to stretch the neck.

While some people spend their lives dieting to reduce their body size, others spend most of their time exercising to increase it. Body builders treat their bodies rather like a living sculpture, building up muscle strength and size through weight-training and exercise.

*C*utting & tucking

Today, the craft of the plastic surgeon has put ancient body-shaping techniques in the shade. It is now possible for people to have virtually every part of their body altered. Excess fat is removed through a technique called liposuction, breasts are enlarged, entire faces are reshaped and wrinkles are treated with Botox injections. By far the most widespread surgical enhancement, however, is the facelift. In an era in which youth is seen as all-important, an increasing number of women and men are regularly submitting their faces to the scalpel.

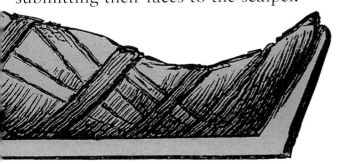

*P*LASTIC FANTASTIC

Like many stars, the American singer and actress Cher (b.1946) has undergone plastic surgery, having her nose reshaped and her face lifted.

Tooth & nail

MANY A BEAUTY'S SMILE WAS MARRED by rotten or missing teeth before the 19th century, when modern dental science began to develop and people began to understand the causes of tooth decay. In the past, the cheapest solution was to have rotten teeth extracted – an excruciatingly painful business before anaesthetics were invented in the 1840s.

Teething problems

The first-known sets of false teeth were made in Italy around 2,700 years ago, by the Etruscans. The use of dentures had died out by the Middle Ages, however, and when they were reintroduced in the 17th century, only the wealthy could afford them. More ornamental than practical, early dentures often fell out and had to be removed when eating.

What a mouthful

Early false teeth were carved from animal bone, ivory or mother-of-pearl, or cast in silver or gold. Human teeth were also used – pulled from the dead or sold by poor people from their own mouths.

Cultural differences

Not everyone thinks that even, glistening white teeth are beautiful. In parts of Africa and Southeast Asia, teeth are filed into sharp points or dyed different colours.

Mouth jewellery

Decorating teeth with precious jewels is not a new custom. Hundreds of years ago, the Mayan people of South America inlaid their teeth with turquoise and jade.

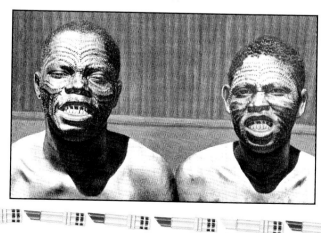

In China, it was once the custom for noblewomen to grow their nails to as long as 25 centimetres. Sometimes the nails were sheathed in gold or silver to protect them.

Hands-on experience

Throughout history, clean hands and buffed, filed fingernails were considered a sign of the leisured upper classes. At times it was also fashionable for the aristocracy to show that they didn't dirty their hands with work by growing extremely long nails.

Nail varnish didn't come on to the market until the mid-1920s, when it was sold alongside the new, mass-produced make-up. Open-toed sandals became fashionable at this time, and women started to paint their toenails. In the 1930s, it became stylish to co-ordinate nail varnish and lipstick colours.

The 1980s was the age of power dressing, and no well-groomed career women looked complete without immaculate nails. Once a service offered only by hair salons, manicure parlours sprouted in high streets and shopping malls, offering everything from a lunchtime retouch to a full set of false nails.

TAKING FINE FINGERNAILS

Although artificial nails didn't become a fashion accessory until the 1970s, they were marketed to nail-biters as early as the 1930s. These days they're available in a range of colours and decorations.

Hairy faces

MEN'S MOUSTACHES AND BEARDS *have come and gone over the centuries. Ancient Egyptian men were usually clean-shaven, for example, although beards were fashionable from time to time.*

Splitting hairs

In ancient Greece, in contrast, beards were usual until the 5th century BCE, after which they were mainly worn only by old men and philosophers as a sign of their freedom from worldly concerns. The Romans were obsessed with a clean shave, and no man's day was complete without a morning visit to the barber. Viking men, on the other hand, wouldn't have been seen dead without a beard.

When beards and moustaches were in, men often rang the changes by altering their shape. For the noblemen of medieval Europe, for instance, a neatly trimmed and waxed forked beard was stylish for many decades.

FACIAL FALSIE

Like other ancient Egyptians, pharaohs were usually clean shaven. However, part of their royal regalia was a false beard tied around the chin with a strap.

MAKING A POINT

Upturned moustache tips and a goatee beard were all the rage in the first half of the 17th century.

VICTORIAN VALUES

As the 19th century progressed, luxuriant facial hair came to symbolize the Victorian ideals of seriousness and sobriety. The second man from the left's sideburns were a new fashion.

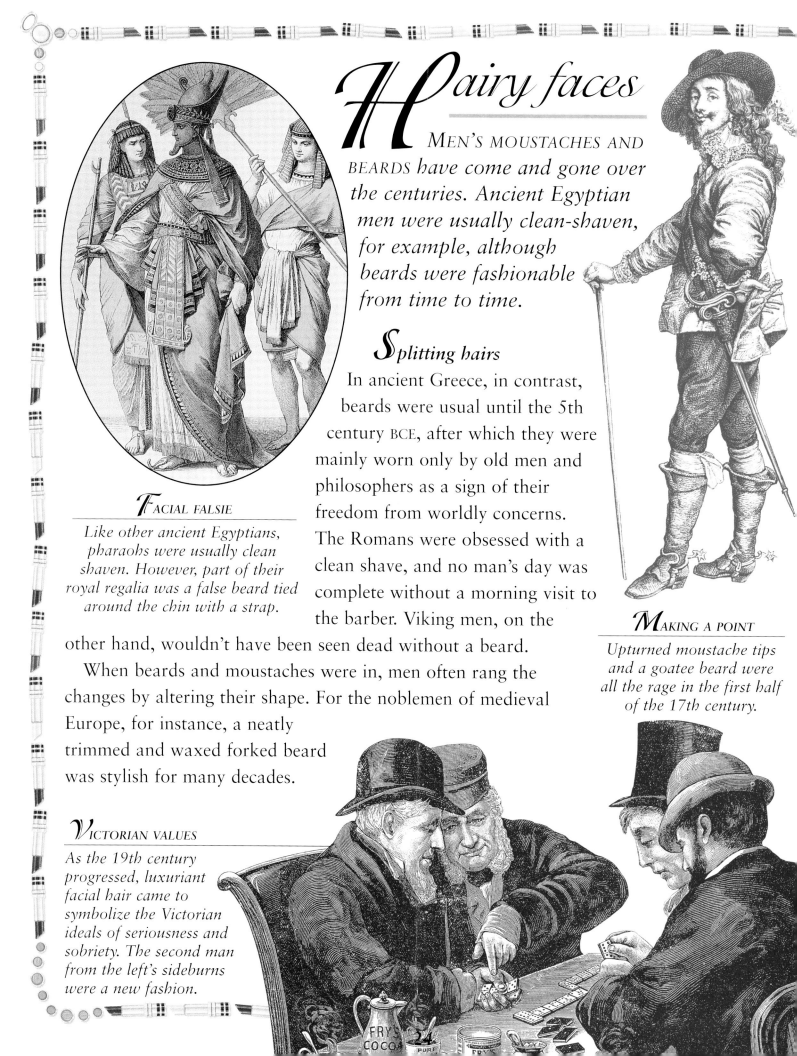

HOLY HAIR

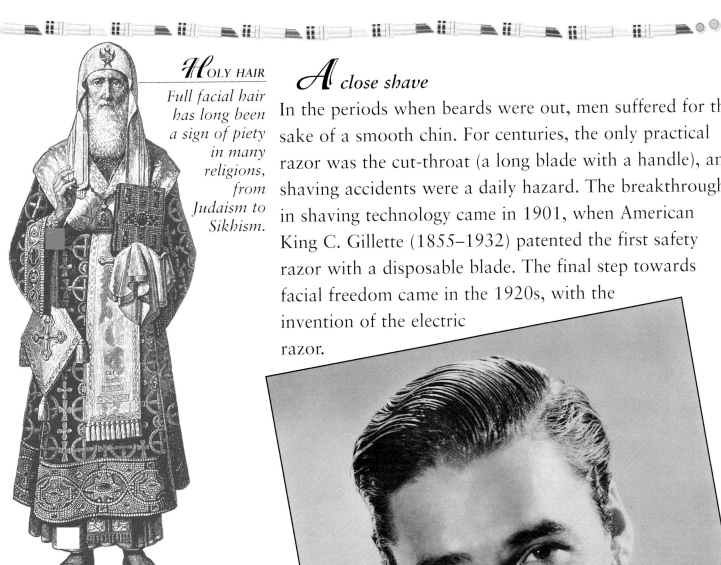

Full facial hair has long been a sign of piety in many religions, from Judaism to Sikhism.

A close shave

In the periods when beards were out, men suffered for the sake of a smooth chin. For centuries, the only practical razor was the cut-throat (a long blade with a handle), and shaving accidents were a daily hazard. The breakthrough in shaving technology came in 1901, when American King C. Gillette (1855–1932) patented the first safety razor with a disposable blade. The final step towards facial freedom came in the 1920s, with the invention of the electric razor.

DESIGNER STUBBLE

In the 1980s, film and pop icons such as singer George Michael (b.1963) set a trend for designer stubble.

LIP STYLE

A pencil-thin moustache became a must for men in the 1930s, after the style was sported by movie stars such as the swashbuckling Errol Flynn (right, 1909–59) and the suave Clark Gable (1901–60).